Also available in the
26 FAIRMOUNT AVENUE series:

26 Fairmount Avenue
a 2000 Newbery Honor Book
Here We All Are
On My Way
What a Year

THE WAR YEARS:

Things Will NEVER Be the Same
I'm Still Scared

WHY?

written and illustrated by

Tomie dePaola

A 26 FAIRMOUNT AVENUE BOOK

G. P. Putnam's Sons

G. P. PUTNAM'S SONS A division of Penguin Young Readers Group. Published by The Penguin Group. Penguin Group (USA) Inc., 375 Hudson Street, New York, NY 10014, U.S.A. Penguin Group (Canada), 90 Eglinton Avenue East, Suite 700, Toronto, Ontario, Canada M4P 2Y3 (a division of Pearson Penguin Canada Inc.). Penguin Books Ltd, 80 Strand, London WC2R 0RL, England. Penguin Ireland, 25 St. Stephen's Green, Dublin 2, Ireland (a division of Penguin Books Ltd.). Penguin Group (Australia), 250 Camberwell Road, Camberwell, Victoria 3124, Australia (a division of Pearson Australia Group Pty Ltd). Penguin Books India Pvt Ltd, 11 Community Centre, Panchsheel Park, New Delhi - 110 017, India. Penguin Group (NZ), Cnr Airborne and Rosedale Roads, Albany, Auckland 1310, New Zealand (a division of Pearson New Zealand Ltd). Penguin Books (South Africa) (Pty) Ltd, 24 Sturdee Avenue, Rosebank, Johannesburg 2196, South Africa. Penguin Books Ltd, Registered Offices: 80 Strand, London WC2R 0RL, England.

Published simultaneously in Canada. Printed in the United States of America. Book design by Marikka Tamura. Text set in Garth Graphic. Library of Congress Cataloging-in-Publication Data De Paola, Tomie. Why? : the war years / written and illustrated by Tomie dePaola. p. cm. — (A 26 Fairmount Avenue Book) 1. De Paola, Tomie—Childhood and youth—Juvenile literature. 2. De Paola, Tomie—Homes and haunts—Connecticut—Meriden—Juvenile literature. 3. Connecticut—Intellectual life—20th century—Juvenile literature. 4. Authors, American—20th century—Biography—Juvenile literature. 5. Meriden (Conn.)—Social life and customs—Juvenile literature. 6. Illustrators. 7. Illustrators—United States—Biography. I. Title. II. Series: De Paola, Tomie. 26 Fairmount Avenue book. PS3554.E11474Z4787   2007   813'.54—dc22 [B] 2006011911 ISBN 978-0-399-24692-0

1 3 5 7 9 10 8 6 4 2

First Impression

*For all the families in the world who lost loved ones
in those first days of WWII.*

Chapter One

January 1, New Year's Day, 1942

Dear NEW Diary,

Welcome to my life.
I will try to write in you
every day!
1942 — Y.B.F.I.T.W.
TOMIE

Mom and Dad had a New Year's Eve party last night. Everyone had a good time even though we are at war. Mom let me stay up until midnight. We all stood around the radio waiting for the New Year to be announced. I remembered when our family had listened to the radio together just a few weeks before, when President Roosevelt said that the Japanese had bombed Pearl Harbor in Hawaii on December 7. That was the beginning of World War II for America.

Tonight was different. We were listening to the crowds in Times Square in New York City. Every year, for a long time, a big ball covered with lightbulbs would fall down a big pole that was way up on the top of the *New York Times* building. Lots of people would fill the streets, shouting, "Nine, eight, seven . . ."

We did the same thing at 26 Fairmount Avenue. ". . . six, five, four, three, two, one! Happy New Year!"

We blew horns and other noisemakers
that Uncle Charles and his girlfriend, Viva,
had brought. They gave Buddy and Maureen
and me party hats. (Of course, Maureen was
in bed, but she'd wear her party hat all the
next day.)

Uncle Charles was not wearing an Army uniform like we thought he would. He found out that it would be a couple of months before he was "officially" in the Army. Buddy wore his new Boy Scout uniform, though.

"I want to show everyone that I'm patriotic," he said. I think that meant that he loves America.

I wore a white shirt and a necktie.

So many of our friends were there: Vinnie and his girlfriend, Queenie; Mickey Lynch; Mr. Bob Dowling and his girlfriend, Edna; Mr. Joe Suma and his girlfriend, Monnie; Carol Crane's mother and father, Helen and Frank; and Roy and Yvonne Brooks. Carol Crane and Bobby Brooks, who was Buddy's age, were there, too. Besides Uncle Charles and his girlfriend, Viva, some of our other

4

have to go into the Army. Someone [...] at there would be shortages of lots of [...]s. Someone else, I think it was Cousin [...]el's voice, said, "Oh, come on. This war [...]n't last long. You'll see."

[...]uddenly I saw Mom coming toward the [...]airs. "I'm going to look in on Maureen," [...]he said. She almost caught me. I couldn't get inside my room, so I turned around. I yawned and rubbed my eyes.

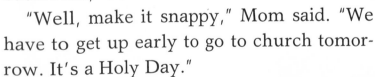

"Tomie, what are you doing up?" Mom asked.

"I have to go to the bathroom," I said.

"Well, make it snappy," Mom said. "We have to get up early to go to church tomorrow. It's a Holy Day."

Before I climbed into bed, I looked out the frosty bedroom window. It was so dark out there, with only a few streetlights lit. Even

relatives were there: Cousin Mabel and her husband, Bill Powers; Uncle Nick, my dad's brother, and Aunt Loretta, his wife; and Mom's cousin Ed Downey and his wife, Kay.

Mom had made sandwiches with the crusts cut off. Dad had filled a big platter with Italian stuff that everyone liked. I helped Mom make celery stalks stuffed with cream cheese mixed with cherry juice and some others stuffed with cream cheese and green olives. All the grown-ups had drinks. We kids had Cokes with ice.

"Well, we're going to make sure that this will be a great party, because we won't know about next year," Mom told everyone.

Then we heard the radio announcer say, "Happy 1942, radio listeners. The festivities from Times Square were especially crowded this year. The famous New Year's Ball will be put in mothballs (that meant "in storage") until the war is over. Let's all hope that that is soon!"

The Crane and Brooks families said good night and left.

Buddy went upstairs. So, I was sent off to bed, too. Buddy was already asleep when I came into our bedroom to put my pajamas on.

I could hear everyone still laughing and talking. I went down the hall and into the bathroom and brushed my teeth. When I finished, I crept out into the hall.

I had a "secret" way of watching and listening to everything in the living room. I'd lie down on the hall floor above the top step

of the stairs an~~d~~
between the top
see everything a~~t~~.
able to see anyone
so I could sneak away
to my room.

Now the grown-ups
They talked about the ene~~r~~
the draft, which meant that
would have to get a number ~~t~~
draft board, and if their numbe~~r~~

they'd
said t~~h~~
thing
Mab
wo~~n~~

st
s

if people were still up, like at our house, you couldn't see any lit windows in the houses because of all the blackout curtains we had to close every night so enemy planes wouldn't see anything if they flew over.

There was one more weekend before school started up again. It had snowed, so we kids would be able to spend some fun time sliding at Del Favaros' field. Saturday, I'd be able to go down to Wallingford with Dad and Buddy to help out at Tom and

Nana's grocery store. Dancing School wouldn't start until the next week. And of course on Sunday, after we had Sunday dinner, we'd go visit Tom and Nana at their house like we did almost every Sunday.

Even though lots of things have changed because of the war, there are still some things that are just the same. I like that!

Chapter Two

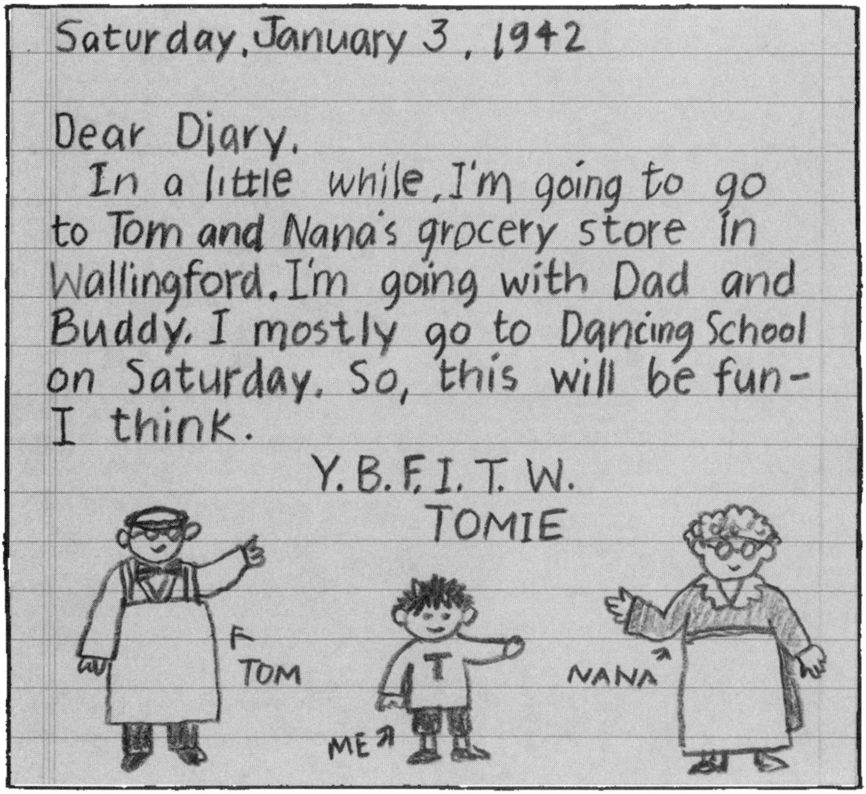

Saturday, January 3, 1942

Dear Diary,
  In a little while, I'm going to go to Tom and Nana's grocery store in Wallingford. I'm going with Dad and Buddy. I mostly go to Dancing School on Saturday. So, this will be fun— I think.
                    Y. B. F. I. T. W.
                         TOMIE

TOM   ME   NANA

While we were eating breakfast, my grand-father Tom called on the telephone and asked Dad to pick up some stuff at the Armour meatpacking place. I had never been there

11

before, but I knew that Tom got lots of meat for his store from Armour's. Dad, Buddy, and I went into the office and Dad gave the lady behind the desk the list. She filled out some papers and stamped them with a thing that looked like the one the library used when we took out a book.

"Mr. dePaola," she said, "ask for Jerry. He handles Mr. Downey's account, so he knows the kind of quality Mr. Downey likes. Go right through these doors."

"Bundle up, boys," Dad said. "It's going to be cold in there."

Dad pulled my hat down over my ears. We went through a set of double doors and Dad rang a doorbell.

A big door clanked open and cold air and steam rushed out at us. The door shut with a thud. We were in a very large room that was icy cold. I could see my breath. The

floor was covered with sawdust, and hanging from hooks on the walls and ceiling were big pieces of meat.

"The big ones are called 'sides of beef,'" Dad explained. "Those over there are lamb, and way over there is the pork."

Big barrels filled with slabs of corned beef, pickled pigs' feet and other weird-looking stuff were scattered around the room. Some of the men, called butchers, were cutting the big sides of meat into halves or smaller pieces at thick wooden tables.

"Hi, I'm Jerry," said a man wearing a white coat over his overcoat. He had on a hat, earmuffs, and heavy shoes. All the men were dressed the same.

"This is just like Tom's walk-in cooler at the store," Buddy whispered. "Only it's lots bigger."

Jerry looked through the big sides of beef hanging from the ceiling. He lifted one down and put it on one of the wooden tables. It was almost as big as Dad.

He made some marks on it, then took it to a big electric saw. Another man helped him. They sawed the beef in half the long way and then sawed one of the halves into two pieces. They wrapped both pieces in the same white paper Tom used in the store. They taped both packages shut and wrote "Downey" on them with a black crayon like Tom's.

Jerry looked over the lamb. He grabbed one and wrapped it up without sawing it in pieces.

Then he fished out
some slabs of corned
beef from the barrel
and wrapped them
in several layers of
paper so the pack-
age wouldn't leak.
Finally he pulled some
pigs' feet from their barrel
and put them in a large cardboard tub.

"Why don't you move your car around
back and we can load it right up," Jerry told
Dad.

"Sonny," Jerry said, looking at me, "be
sure to watch your grandfather turn all this
meat into steaks and lamb chops. He's a real
artist! Maybe you'll grow up to be a butcher,
too," he added.

"My name is Tomie," I said. "I am going
to be an artist when I grow up, only an artist
with paints and crayons and stuff."

"Well, good for you. Be sure to tell Mr.
Downey that Jerry said hello. Oops. I almost
forgot the case of frankfurters."

It took only a half hour to get to Wallingford. We pulled into the big parking lot behind the store and went in the back door. Dad, Buddy, Uncle Charles, and Tom unloaded the car.

Tom opened the door to the walk-in cooler. I peeked inside. Chickens ready for cooking were hanging from hooks on the walls, next to a couple of sides of beef and lamb. There was a barrel just like at Armour's filled with corned beef, and tubs of pigs' feet. Cases of frankfurters filled the shelves against the wall. Near the door was another barrel with a large fork tied to it. Tom fished into the barrel and brought up a big juicy dill pickle.

"Here's a tip for you, me bucko," Tom said. "Go sit down at the desk and eat it before you get to work."

I had three jobs. The first was to stand on the counter and put cans of vegetables on the shelves.

"Nice and neat, with the labels facing out," Nana said.

Next, because I had good handwriting, I had to mark the cans that were ON SALE with the special price. I used one of Tom's black crayons. Then I stacked them up on a table, just like my wooden blocks.

My third job was the most fun. I had to pick the best potatoes from the big basket and put them into bags, four or five in each, depending on the size. Next,  I tied up the bags the way Nana showed me, with the string that was above the scale. Then I weighed them and wrote very clearly how much they weighed.

Meanwhile, Buddy and Dad helped Uncle Charles "put up" the orders. "Four cans of Del Monte peas for Mrs. Lahey. Two bags of potatoes. One head of cabbage." The last thing to go in each order was the meat. "A nice fat roasting chicken, two pounds of ground chuck, one pound of liverwurst, and a nice soup bone," Nana would announce to Tom, who was *always* behind the meat counter at the back of the store.

The orders lined the counter, waiting for the packages of meat. Once the boxes were all set, they were put in the back of my grandfather's black Ford truck and Uncle Charles and Buddy would deliver them. Dad put some orders in the trunk and on the backseat of his car. He would go by himself to deliver them.

Nana said I was too small to go. I think she was afraid I'd sing one of my songs at every house, "just like Cousin Morton did when he was your age."

While the morning orders were being delivered, I had my lunch. I picked out one of my favorite "cold cuts," which was what we called bologna, luncheon loaf, salami, boiled ham, and stuff like that. Nana would make me a sandwich with "Iowa State

butter," "Cains mayonnaise," and "French's mustard." They were her favorites.

If Tom made my sandwich, he would use *his* favorites—"Land O'Lakes butter," "Hellman's mayonnaise" and "Gulden's mustard." Tom would always give me another dill pickle from the pickle barrel.

For dessert, I'd have a Mrs. Frisbie's "nickel" pie. It was about four inches wide and was usually apple, cherry, or peach. Mrs. Frisbie's bakery was in Bridgeport. They made two sizes of pies, the small nickel ones and the regular eight-inch ones. They were in metal pie plates and came in waxed paper bags. The pies actually cost six cents, but you got a penny back when you returned the "nickel" size plate. I don't know how much you got back when you returned the big pie plate. We NEVER had a Mrs. Frisbie's pie for our family dessert, only a small pie when we worked at the store.

I ate my lunch at the big rolltop desk in the back of the store. Then I watched Tom work at his "butcher table," cutting up lamb

chops and steaks and—my favorite thing to watch—cleaning the chickens.

Tom had given me chicken feet to take home as a joke. He showed me how to loosen the tendon on each foot and to pull it. When I did, the chicken foot opened and closed as if it were alive. I was forbidden to take chicken feet to school. I did once and scared a teacher. That was the end of that!

When Buddy, Dad, and Uncle Charles got back, there were some more orders to put up. Once that was done, Dad would deliver them in Tom's truck.

Uncle Charles would take us up the street to Charlie's Smoke Shop. On the way we'd stop off and say hello to his girlfriend, Viva. She worked at Gallagher Brothers Coal and Oil Company on Saturdays. Then, we'd go into Charlie's and Buddy and I could each pick out five comic books.

Buddy's favorites were *Superman, Batman, The Green Hornet, Dick Tracy, Buck Rogers, Joe Palooka,* comics like that! MY favorites were *Little Lulu, The Pie-faced Prince of Pretzelburg, Fairy Tale Parade, Classic Comics, Mickey Mouse, Nancy,* and other funny comics. It would be a while before I liked adventure comics.

Finally, it was time to get ready to go home. Nana had put up our order and Tom had wrapped our chicken and meat for the

week. Sometimes he'd draw pictures on the packages. It was always fun to open everything up when we got home.

I'd think to myself, *I wonder what kind of butter we got this week, Iowa State or Land O'Lakes?* We usually got both. I think Tom would sneak the Land O'Lakes into our box without Nana knowing.

"Well, Timothy," Tom said to me as we were leaving (he gave me two nicknames—me bucko and Timothy), "you tell your mom that next year, you have your dancing lesson after school. I like you here helping me out. Why, I might even teach you to clean chickens! See you tomorrow." (We always went to Tom and Nana's house on Sunday.) "We'll go to Mr. Foote's and get ice cream."

Not a single person had even mentioned the war.

Chapter Three

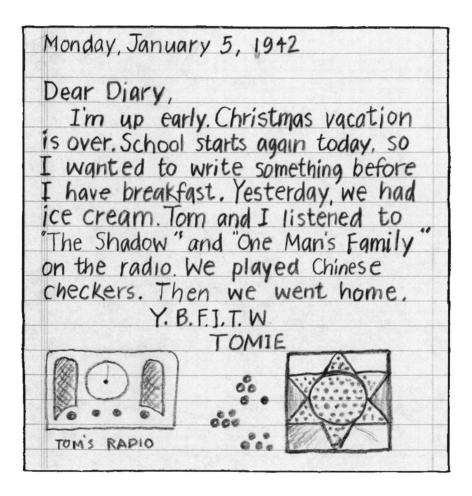

Monday, January 5, 1942

Dear Diary,
   I'm up early. Christmas vacation is over. School starts again today, so I wanted to write something before I have breakfast. Yesterday, we had ice cream. Tom and I listened to "The Shadow" and "One Man's Family" on the radio. We played Chinese checkers. Then we went home.
                Y. B. F. I. T. W
                   TOMIE

TOM'S RADIO

"Boys." It was Mom standing in the doorway.

I closed my diary and sat up in bed. Buddy groaned and rolled over.

"The morning paper says that parents should make sure their children will be dressed extra warm this morning. The schools will be using less coal while we are at war. So the heat will be lowered and it will be colder in your classrooms. Tomie, you wear that green zip-up sweater over your shirt and undershirt. Buddy, you're old enough to decide for yourself. Come down as quickly as you can so you can have a good breakfast."

Buddy was always slower than I was in the morning. So by the time I washed up and went back to the bedroom to dress, Buddy's feet were just hitting the floor. The smell of pancakes was in the air. I dressed quickly and ran downstairs.

Sure enough, there on the table was a stack of pancakes and a pitcher of Log Cabin maple syrup. Mom put three on my plate, buttered them

(was it Iowa State or Land O'Lakes?), and put the syrup in front of me.

"Don't use up all the syrup, now. Leave enough for Buddy," Mom told me.

Maureen was already in her high chair, eating a pancake with her fingers.

"And look—a surprise for the first day of school of the New Year!" Mom was holding a bottle of milk. The cream on top had frozen and pushed up the cap. This happened lots in the winter, well, not lots, but a couple of times. When I first saw the frozen cream, I thought Mom had bought ice cream with the milk.

Mom scooped a spoonful into a cup for me. It was cold and crunchy, even better than ice cream as far as I was concerned. If Miss Gardner has us stand and tell the best part of our vacation, I'll tell everyone about the frozen cream on the milk.

Buddy and I finished our breakfast and ran down snowy Fairmount Avenue, turning down Highland Avenue to catch our ride with Mr. Houdlette, Jeannie's father.

"Good thing you boys made it this morning," Mr. Houdlette said. "It's pretty cold out there."

In fact, it was so cold that Mr. Houdlette dropped Buddy, Jeannie, and me off at the corner of King Street, where the school was, instead of at the corner of Hanover and Orange, which was four blocks away. He never did that!

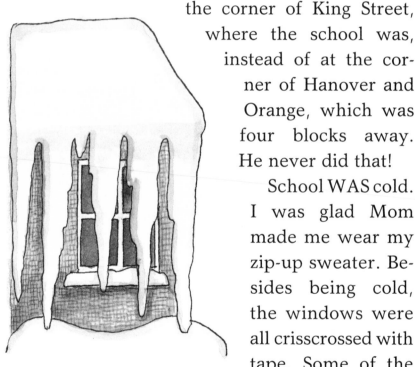

School WAS cold. I was glad Mom made me wear my zip-up sweater. Besides being cold, the windows were all crisscrossed with tape. Some of the kids swore they could see their breath, but really, it wasn't THAT cold.

Our second-grade teacher, Miss Gardner, rang the little bell on her desk. This meant Quiet.

"Good morning, boys and girls, and happy New Year. I hope you all had a very nice holiday. First, let's pledge allegiance to the flag."

We all stood and recited the pledge. Then we sang "My Country 'Tis of Thee."

"Everyone, sit, please. Now, I notice a few of you children aren't wearing an extra sweater or something warm. We have a box of extra things up here by my desk. Don't be shy and don't worry if things are too big or too small."

Several of my classmates filed up and tried on the extra sweaters.

I noticed that Miss Fisher, the teacher across the hall, had on her outside coat. She wasn't wearing her hat, though.

"I suppose you are all wondering why the windows are criss-crossed with tape. Well, it's a precaution. If a bomb drops, the glass will not shatter and spray all over the place. The tape will help hold the glass in place," Miss Gardner said.

Suddenly the air raid drill bell rang.

"Line up for our air raid drill," Miss Gardner said.

We lined up quickly. I looked around. Some of the kids looked scared. I had a jumpy feeling in my stomach.

Miss Fisher came across the hall and whispered to Miss Gardner, "I didn't know we were going to have a drill."

"Go back to your class. I'm sure it's all right," Miss Gardner whispered back.

We all heard her.

The second bell rang. We filed down to the basement. Some kids forgot where we were supposed to go. It was very confusing. Some younger kids started to cry. The teachers tried to calm everyone down.

We were in the shelter area for a long time, or at least it felt like a long time. One

thing that I noticed was the furnace wasn't hissing as loud as it was during the first air raid drill.

Finally the bell rang again.

"All right, boys and girls, that was the all clear," Miss Burke, the principal, announced. "You may go back to your classrooms."

When Buddy, Jeannie, and I walked home for lunch, I asked Buddy if he thought it was a REAL air raid, and was he scared?

"Naw," he said. "I knew it was only a drill."

"How come?" I asked.

"You didn't hear any planes, did you? How can you have a real air raid, with bombs dropping, if there aren't any planes?"

Well, I guess he was right.

Mom had our favorite lunch, cream of tomato soup and grilled cheese sandwiches.

In the afternoon, school was back to normal except it was still a little bit cold.

"This afternoon, class," Miss Gardner said, "we are going to begin penmanship. When I call your name, come up to my desk and I will give you an empty ink bottle that goes in the little hole at the top right hand side of your desk. I will also give you a penholder and a pen point. Take good care of them because they are School Property."

Just like everything in this room, I thought.

After we were back at our desks, we put the empty ink bottles in the holes in our desks.

Jack and Warren S. were named ink monitors. They went up and down the aisles and poured the ink Miss Gardner had made from powder and water into the inkwells. Patty passed out the penmanship paper. It was white with blue lines on it. Miss Gardner explained how to put the pen point into the penholder.

"Please watch," Miss Gardner said. She drew lines on the blackboard just like Mr. Conklin did for music. Only these lines were blue.

"What we have to do first is to learn our Palmer Method exercises. Now, watch me carefully." Miss Gardner took a piece of white chalk and began to go up and down and forward.

Next she made circles.

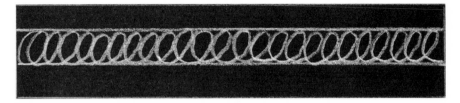

Then she made loops.

"Now," Miss Gardner continued, "hold your pen in your right hand between your thumb and your first finger. Dip the pen point gently in your ink and copy the exercises five times each on your paper."

I was in lots of trouble. First of all, I couldn't hold the pen right. It went all over the paper. If I held it with my first two fin-

gers and thumb, then it was okay. I hoped Miss Gardner wouldn't notice.

Then, the pen point got "stuck" in the paper and ink went all over the place. I tried again and this time I had too much ink on the pen point and it left a "LAKE" on my paper.

I looked around the room. Some of the kids were doing just fine. The "lefties," kids who used their left hands, were having an even harder time than I was.

I kept hoping we'd have another air raid drill.

Chapter Four

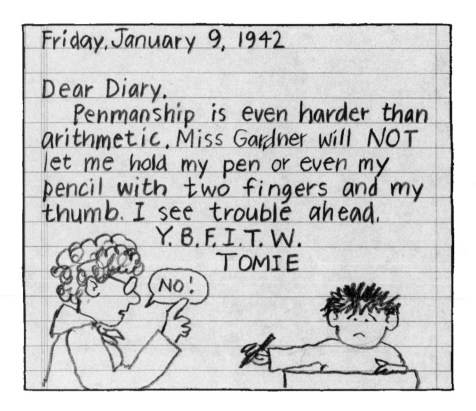

Today was the worst day since school started this year. Miss Gardner took adhesive tape and taped my three fingers together so I can't hold my pen with two fingers and my thumb. My "exercises" are all over the place. And I don't know WHO invented those pen points. They splurt and catch in the paper. The way Miss Gardner fusses over them, I'll bet that if I broke one, I'd go to jail.

Mom said she'd help me. She bought me a penholder and a small box of pen points. The lady at Jepson's stationery store told Mom to hold the pen points over a flame to make them stronger. We'll see if that works.

At least the week had one sunshiny day. My first issue of *Children's Playmate* magazine came in the mail on Wednesday.

When I was younger, I got *Wee Wisdom*, but then as I got older, it got boring. The stories weren't very interesting and there was a lot of stuff about how to be polite and things like that.

Children's Playmate has a color cover and I think the same artist does the picture every month. She signs it Fern Bisel Peat. Mom said that she is the "Art Director," and she picks

out all the art in the magazine. There are good
stories, too. On the four pages in the middle
of the magazine, there is a paper doll page.

I'll confess a secret. I like paper dolls.

Jeannie gets paper doll books at the five-
and-dime stores. But boys aren't supposed
to play with paper dolls. I cheat!

I draw clothes for Jeannie's paper dolls.
I like putting the little tabs at the shoulders
and waist. In a box in our playroom in the

attic, I'm keeping some paper dolls that I am making myself. I'm getting lots of ideas from the costume books that Miss Leah has at Dancing School. Miss Leah lets me look through the costume and material books. She knows I'll be very careful!

In *Children's Playmate* two of the pages have drawings and photos by children from all over the country. You send in something and if Miss Fern Bisel Peat likes it, they publish it (I guess).

The magazine says it's also a good way to "have a pen pal." Mom says that a pen pal is someone who becomes your friend by writing letters back and forth. That sounds like fun. Maybe I'll try it.

But meanwhile, I have to work on my PENMANSHIP. I don't think Mr. Palmer liked children very much. If he did, his "drills" would have been more fun.

Tuesday, January 13, 1942

Dear Diary,
   Dad told us at supper that there will be no NEW cars built until the war is over. The car factories are going to build tanks and trucks and a new special car for the war called a JEEP.
   I'm glad Dad got a new car before Pearl Harbor.
                Y. B. F. I. T. W.
                     TOMIE

This is a drawing of the original "Jeep" ⟹
from Popeye.
I got a toy one, Christmas, 1939.

Sunday night, January 18, 1942

Dear Diary,
 Tom and Nana and Mom and Dad were sitting around Nana's dining room table. They were talking low so we kids wouldn't hear.
 I pretended to be busy playing with the blocks so I could listen.
 They were talking about this thing called rationing. Nana said if the war goes on, things will get scarce — that means hard to buy. Tom said that there would be rationing like in World War I.
 I wonder what kinds of things will get scarce?
                   Y.B.F.I.T.W.
                   TOMIE

CANDY?   CRAYONS?   BOOKS?   GOLDFISH?

Wednesday, January 21, 1942

Dear Diary,
    Well, I'm the Last one in my class who hasn't lost a tooth. Most kids lost at least ONE tooth in Kindergarten or First Grade. Yesterday, Nancy lost her bottom tooth, so I'm left.
    Jeannie has two beautiful permanent teeth. She thinks they are too big, but I wish I had them.
    Buddy said that it proves I'm just a baby! If he was my younger brother and not my older one, I'd be nice to him.
                    Y.B.F.I.T.W.
                        TOMIE

Monday, January 26, 1942

Dear Diary,
   Our cousin, Anthony is coming to visit. His nickname is Blackie because he has black hair and black eyes. Everyone likes him and he has a white, white smile.
   He likes me a lot. He lets me ride on his shoulders and always asks me what new song I know. I'll be able to sing "We're the Couple in the Castle" for him. That's our song for Miss Leah's recital.
   Blackie is in the ARMY AIR CORPS. He's coming on Friday.
                    Y. B. F. I. T. W.
                       TOMIE

← BLACKIE   ME →

Chapter Five

Sunday night, February 1, 1942

Dear Diary,
   Cousin Blackie went back to the Bronx tonight. Everybody came to 26 Fairmount Avenue for a party, even Tom and Nana.
   Blackie brought ME two—2— presENTS, a Hawaiian guitar and a grass skirt!
   He said he is going to fight the NAZIS.
                    Y.B.F.I.T.W.
                       TOMIE

What a weekend! The house was crowded with people. Aunt Kate, Uncle Tony, and our cousins Theresa (Blackie's younger sister),

Dominic (Blackie's younger brother), and Blackie all came up to Connecticut from the Bronx.

Everyone came to the party because Blackie was on his way to the war in Europe. He was in the Hawaiian Islands when the Japanese bombed Pearl Harbor. But he wasn't on the island the Japanese attacked. Blackie was lucky.

Now they need bomber gunners in Europe to fly over to Germany, where the war is. Blackie is a Belly Gunner. "I'm short," he said, "so I fit easily into the bubble under the bomber. That's why they call us the Belly Gunners."

Blackie brought us kids presents from Hawaii.

I was so excited when I opened up a genuine Hawaiian guitar just for me. It had a book with it. Blackie showed me how to play it a little. Then I opened up a big box. Inside was a genuine grass skirt with a hat made out of grass, too.

"That's a good present for a sissy," Buddy whispered to me.

But Blackie heard him. "Hey, Buddy, this is a grass skirt for a man dancer. Men wear grass skirts when they do certain ceremonial dances."

So there! I knew what my Halloween costume would be.

Friday night, we had Blackie all to ourselves. While the grown-ups were sitting at the kitchen table talking after supper, Blackie sat with me in the living room and asked me how everything was. I told him about the Palmer Method and how Mom said she'd help me.

"Oh, boy, if Aunt Floss is going to help you, you have nothing to worry about. She's so smart, she can do almost anything. I'll tell you a secret," Blackie said, lowering his voice. "She's my favorite aunt. Don't tell anybody!"

I said I wouldn't.

We talked some more and I sang "We're the Couple in the Castle" for him and told him how Carol Morrissey was my partner and Patty Clark was Billy Burns's partner. Then I told him about being the only one in second grade who still had all his BABY teeth.

"Let me see," Blackie said. "Open up."

I opened my mouth wide. Blackie looked inside. Then he put his finger on one of my bottom teeth and he moved it back and forth.

"I think this one is a little loose. Try it."

I put my finger on my tooth and moved it. It seemed a little loose.

On Saturday, Uncle Nick, Aunt Loretta, and their daughter, Cousin Helen, came over. And Uncle Frank, Aunt Susie, Aunt Clo, and Cousins Frances and Connie drove down from Fall River. Nana Fall-River came, too.

"We thought we'd better come for a visit before the government starts rationing gas," Uncle Frank said. They all stayed at Uncle Nick's house.

Everyone was there for Sunday dinner. Tom and Nana, Uncle Charles, and his girlfriend, Viva, came up from Wallingford. Nana brought a roasted turkey even though it wasn't Thanksgiving or Christmas. Nana Fall-River brought a big pot of tomato sauce. Dad made meatballs and cooked spaghetti.

Aunt Kate brought cheese and pastries from the Bronx and Uncle Nick and Aunt Loretta brought antipasto—cold cuts, cheeses, peppers, and olives. Tom brought ice cream from Foote's. It was a real feast.

I'd have a lot to tell my friends at school tomorrow.

Chapter Five

Tuesday, February 3, 1942

Dear Diary,
    Mrs. Bowers, the art teacher, is coming to King Street School tomorrow.
Hooray!
            Y.B.F.I.T.W.
                TOMIE

"Boys and girls," Miss Gardner said, "pick up your chairs quietly and go across the hall to Miss Fisher's room. Mrs. Bowers is here for art and she doesn't have enough time to go to each room. So we will join the other second grade."

I was a little disappointed. I was hoping to have Mrs. Bowers all to myself—well, at least to OUR class. But I guess this is better than nothing.

Miss Fisher's class had made room for us, so there were two of us at each desk. I was lucky. I got to share with Jean M.

"Hello, everyone," Mrs. Bowers said cheerfully. "Today we are going to learn to make . . . VALENTINES!"

I was so excited that I clapped.

"Tommy," Miss Fisher warned. (All the teachers made me spell my name T-o-m-m-y instead of T-o-m-i-e.)

Mrs. Bowers gave each of us a piece of red construction paper. She showed us how to fold it in half carefully and in half again. Then we cut a half-a-heart shape, making sure to leave a little piece at the top to hold it all together. There was a double heart!

"Now I'll show you how you can have a little heart-shaped window to open up."

Mrs. Bowers was like a magician. Everything she did was easy to learn and came out so perfect.

"I think every valentine needs some flowers, so I'm going to show how to draw three different flowers," Mrs. Bowers said.

Crayons and paper were passed out. Mrs. Bowers, who always had a big box of colored chalks with her, went to the blackboard.

"First we will make a daisy," Mrs. Bowers said. "Draw a yellow circle and color it in. Then, using any color you want, put eight puppy-dog-ear shapes around the circle, and you have a daisy!"

We all tried. It was fun.

"Next will be a violet. Make a small yellow dot. Then use a dark blue crayon to outline the petals around the yellow dot. At the top make two rabbit-ear shapes. Then put two lamb ears on either side and an upside-down heart at the bottom. Then color in the five violet petals with light purple."

Those were fun to do!

"Now we will make a rose. With red make a spiral shape. Then put half circles all around the spiral and lightly color it in. I think if you use daisies, violets, and roses together, it will look very pretty.

"Oh," Mrs. Bowers said, "I forgot to show you the different leaves. They are all green. So let's draw a green stem from each flower. Some daisies have feathery leaves like this."

Mrs. Bowers drew lots of little lines.

"Violets have very curvy stems and leaves that look like big hearts." She drew them.

"Roses have very sturdy stems and usually three leaves together on a stem off the main stem. The leaves have little notches on the edges."

Mrs. Bowers was so great! She explained everything really, really well. I couldn't wait to make lots and lots of valentines when we went back to our room.

Only that didn't happen. Miss Gardner had put all kinds of arithmetic problems on the blackboard while we were in Miss Fisher's room having art.

"All right, boys and girls, put away your art projects and crayons," Miss Gardner announced. "It's time for arithmetic. Patty, will you pass out the arithmetic paper? Copy the problems off the board and solve them. Be sure you notice that there is addition, subtraction, division, and multiplication. You will have forty-five minutes."

I carefully began copying the problems, but all of a sudden, I remembered Mrs. Bowers telling us about the different flowers. I didn't want to forget what she said or how she drew them.

I turned my arithmetic paper over and carefully drew first the daisy with its stem and feathery leaves, next the rose and its jagged leaves, and finally the violet with its heart-shaped leaves.

I didn't see Miss Gardner standing next to my desk.

"And just what do you think you are doing, young man?"

"I'm just trying to remember how Mrs. Bowers drew the flowers, so I was using the back of my arithmetic paper, Miss Gardner. I thought the flowers would look nice on the Valentine Mailbox," I added quickly.

"Well, since you did not follow instructions, you certainly won't be making the Valentine Mailbox," Miss Gardner said, looking over the class. "Diane and Nancy will make the mailbox this year."

What was I going to tell Mom? She already got me a box from Tom to be the Valentine Mailbox.

When I got home, I told Mom the whole story.

"Tomie, you know how important arithmetic is, especially to Miss Gardner," Mom said.

"But I told Miss Gardner that I had to practice. I told her I wasn't going to be an 'arithmeticker' when I grow up. I'm going to be an artist," I said.

Mom turned away. I think she was smiling.

"Tomorrow," she said, turning back to me, "you can take the box to school and give it to Diane and Nancy to use. But I also want you to tell Miss Gardner that you will try harder at arithmetic—and penmanship, too!"

So, I don't have a lot to look forward to tomorrow. At least Diane and Nancy are good at arithmetic!

Chapter Seven

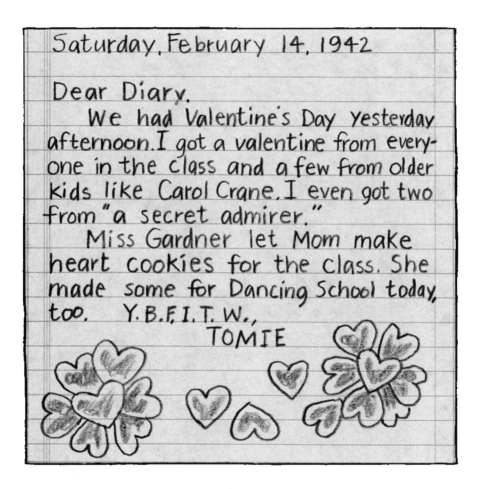

Saturday, February 14, 1942

Dear Diary,
    We had Valentine's Day yesterday afternoon. I got a valentine from everyone in the class and a few from older kids like Carol Crane. I even got two from "a secret admirer."
    Miss Gardner let Mom make heart cookies for the class. She made some for Dancing School today, too.   Y.B.F.I.T.W.,
                    TOMIE

Mom asked Miss Gardner if she could make her heart cookies for Valentine's

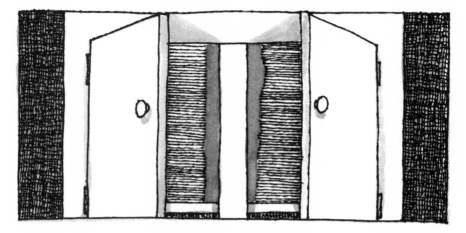

Day. Miss Gardner said something about it maybe being a long time before we have cookies again. Something about "shortages."

Everyone's talking about shortages, shortages. I wish there would be a shortage of arithmetic paper. But I bet Miss Gardner has a huge stack of it "HOARDED" away.

That's another word I've been hearing lately. "Hoarding" is when people get lots of things they think will be scarce—like sugar —and hide it away. I overheard two ladies on the bus talking about a lady who had her husband buy fifty pounds of sugar. They hid it in their basement. But it was damp down there and the whole fifty pounds of sugar turned hard as a rock. So, every night when he came home from work, the husband had to go down to the basement with a hammer and knock off a chunk of sugar for his tea.

Well, it's happened. No more bubble gum! And I just learned how to blow bubbles! Buddy and I went into George's Confectionary Store on our way home from school and right there on the candy counter was a sign:

BECAUSE OF THE WAR, THERE WILL BE NO MORE FLEER'S DOUBLE BUBBLE BUBBLE GUM FOR SALE. George

Mrs. George, who owned George's Confectionary with her husband, told us that it had something to do with the "Japanese and rubber." "I won't be surprised if ALL chewing gum becomes scarce, as well as all the penny candy and of course Hershey bars and the other chocolates. Sugar is going to be rationed VERY SOON."

"How do you think Mrs. George knows this stuff?" I asked Buddy.

"Maybe she's a member of the FBI or something," Buddy answered.

On Saturday afternoon, when I got home from Miss Leah's Dancing School, Buddy couldn't wait to tell me what he had heard Nana and Tom talking about at the store.

"I guess Nana's a member of the FBI, too," he said. "Nana thinks that sugar and butter, meat, and canned goods will be rationed. Tom said tires and gasoline as well as coal and heating oil would be, too. He said that even shoes will probably be rationed because of the leather."

"How come?" I asked.

"For the soldiers," Buddy said. "Soldiers need shoes. They'll need shoes and butter and chocolate and tires—all kinds of stuff."

Sunday, March 8, 1942

Dear Diary,
    Tomorrow is Mom's birthday.
Jeannie is going to help me bake
a cake. It is called a "Hot Milk
Cake." Jeannie has baked a couple
of cakes before, so it will be good!
                    Y.B.F.I.T.W.
                        TOMIE

Wednesday, March 18, 1942

Dear Diary,
I tried to pull out my loose bottom tooth by tying a string to the doorknob. It didn't work. It works in the cartoons, but not for me. Will I ever lose my baby teeth?

Y.B.F.I.T.W.
TOMIE

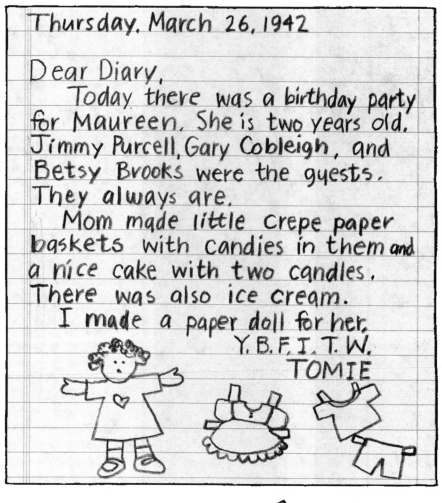

Thursday, March 26, 1942

Dear Diary,
   Today there was a birthday party for Maureen. She is two years old. Jimmy Purcell, Gary Cobleigh, and Betsy Brooks were the guests. They always are.
   Mom made little crepe paper baskets with candies in them and a nice cake with two candles. There was also ice cream.
   I made a paper doll for her.
                    Y.B.F.I.T.W.
                    TOMIE

Saturday, March 28, 1942

Dear Diary,
    Today, Miss Leah asked Billy Burns and me to do a special number in the recital this spring. We will recite a piece about UNCLE SAM.
    "Uncle Sam gets around, but he just don't drift,
    He's a workin' and a givin' everybody a lift."
It is very patriotic.
    Billy and I will stand on either side of the stage and take turns reciting. All the rest of the kids in Dancing School will sing the chorus.
                    Y.B.F.I.T.W.
                    TOMIE

Chapter Eight

Monday, March 30, 1942

Dear Diary,
   Today we aren't going to school. We are going to go to Hartford with Dad. He is going to work and we are going to go shopping at G. Fox and Company with Mom. We are picking out our Easter outfits.

G. FOX   Y. B. F. I. T. W.
                            TOMIE

Hartford is the state capital of Connecticut. It is a big city with a couple of big stores. G. Fox and Company is the biggest. It has escalators. They are moving stairs that take

you from one floor to the next. The elevators are faster, but you get to see more from the escalators. You have to be careful when you get off. The stairs sort of disappear into little slots. There are stories about children whose shoelaces got caught. Mom said it's not true. The only thing is to be careful so you don't fall.

The children's department is up on the eighth floor, so it is a nice long escalator ride. I like looking at all the ladies' dresses, the furniture, the rugs, the lamps, and all the other things. Each floor has different stuff on it.

Finally, we got to the children's department. It is divided into a boys' department, a girls' department, a young man's department, and a young woman's department.

Buddy will get his Easter outfit in the young man's department. I will get mine in the boys' department. We will have to go up another floor to the toddlers' department for Maureen's outfit.

Buddy tried on a pair of long gray flannel  pants and a checkered jacket that is called "tweed." He got a shirt, a clip-on tie, a sweater vest, and new brown shoes. He even got a hat that looks just like the hat my dad wears. It had a little red-and-green feather in the band.

I got a new pair of knickers. I was not old enough for long pants yet. So I got a new pair of knee socks that have a diamond pattern on them. I also got a tweed jacket and a sweater vest. The sweater vest almost matched my

knee socks. I was hoping that Mom would buy me a fedora hat like Buddy's, but I got a tweed cap. I DID get brown-and-white saddle shoes, though.

The clerk told Mom that "next year we'll all need ration stamps for shoes. We've already heard that by fall, ladies' skirts will be shorter, men's pants won't have cuffs on them, and all clothing will have fewer pockets to save material."

We went up to the toddlers' department on the next floor.

The toy department is also on this floor. Mom let me go look at all the toys by myself. There were lots of stuffed animals and teddy bears. Chicks, bunnies, and ducks and very fancy Easter baskets with HUGE

 chocolate rabbits and green cellophane grass were on display for Easter. Games like Uncle Wiggly, Chutes and Ladders, and Monopoly filled the shelves.

There were counters and counters of dolls—very expensive Madame Alexander dolls and Nancy Ann Storybook dolls in their polka dot boxes, all dressed like nursery rhyme characters. Maureen already had a couple of them. They were more to look at than to play with. Several sizes of Dy-Dee dolls that could drink water  from a bottle and then have their diapers changed were next to a whole case of Shirley Temple dolls, all with special costumes from her different movies.

Buddy was looking at the few two-wheelers they had in the toy department.

"Look now, young fella," the clerk said. "These will probably be the last bicycles we'll have until the war is over. There is going to be a shortage of metal and rubber soon."

"Boys," we heard Mom call. "Come see Maureen's Easter outfit." There was Maureen in a pretty white dress with little flowers on it, and a light blue coat with a matching hat that looked like a little bonnet. She was wearing light blue socks and shiny black patent leather Mary Janes.

After we finished shopping, we walked to a big restaurant called De Pasquale's. Dad was waiting for us. We ordered a pizza for lunch and then headed home to Meriden.

As we drove home along the Berlin Turnpike, I kept thinking how nice we'd all look on Easter Sunday at St. Joseph's Church.

Chapter Nine

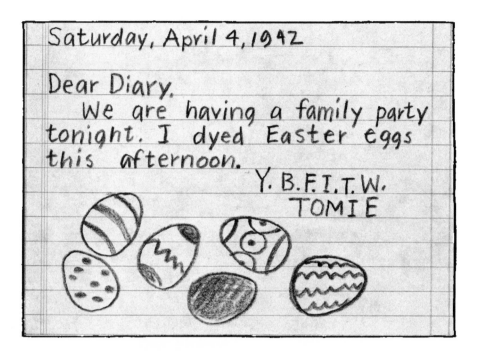

Saturday, April 4, 1942

Dear Diary,
    We are having a family party tonight. I dyed Easter eggs this afternoon.
                        Y. B. F. I. T. W.
                            TOMIE

Uncle Charles got a letter telling him that he had to report for duty on the twelfth of May. So Mom and Dad decided to have a party for him and his girlfriend, Viva, and some of their Wallingford friends.

"The sooner the better," Dad said. "You never know what's going to happen."

The party was the night before Easter Sunday.

Cousin Mabel Powers and her husband, Bill, came, too. Mabel was Mom's favorite cousin. She was a little older than Mom, and her father, Uncle Jack, and Tom were brothers. They lived across the street from the store in Wallingford. I heard some great stories about Cousin Mabel when she and Mom were growing up. Cousin Mabel loved to swim, but without a bathing suit, which was shocking in those days.

So, Mabel and Flossie would walk out into the ocean as far as Flossie could stand. Then Mabel would duck down under the water and take off her bathing suit.

"Here, Flossie," Mabel said. "Hold my bathing suit while I swim out a way." Flossie would stand there and just wait, holding Mabel's suit, until she came back.

"Did you ever think about tricking Cousin Mabel," I asked my mom, "and going back to the beach with her bathing suit?"

"Are you kidding?" Mom said. "She'd have killed me!" And Mom laughed and laughed.

When Cousin Mabel and Bill came in, I whispered to her, "Can I ask you a favor, Cousin Mabel?"

"Sure," she said. "What is it?"

"Well," I told Cousin Mabel, "I'm the only one in my class that hasn't lost a baby tooth yet. Blackie said that my lower front tooth is loose. I wiggle it, and I tried to pull it out with a string tied to a doorknob, but all that happened is the string broke. Can you help me?"

"Let me get some strong string," Mabel said. "Then come with me into the 'Powder Room.'"

We had a small bathroom with a sink and a toilet just off the hallway from the kitchen to the door to the backyard. Mom called 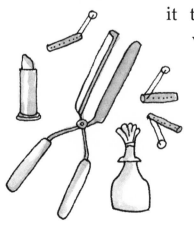 it the Powder Room. It's where she kept her nail polish, her lipsticks and powder and rouge, her hair curlers, and her curling iron. I was especially intrigued with the curling iron. Mom would heat it on the stove, test it out on a folded piece of toilet paper, then, when it was just the right temperature, she'd curl her bangs and fluff them up so they looked soft and pretty!

I secretly (or so I thought) tried it once, but it was too hot, so I had a big burned-out spot right in the front. Mom NEVER mentioned it.

Anyway, Cousin Mabel and I went into the Powder Room. She sat on the closed lid of the toilet seat and tied the string around my loose tooth. She wiggled and tugged gently.

"Does it hurt?" she asked.

"Un-uh," I answered.

Someone knocked on the door. "Go upstairs!" Mabel yelled. "We're busy in here."

She wiggled and tugged. It went on for a long time. And to tell the truth, it was beginning to hurt.

"You okay?" Mabel asked, noticing the tears in my eyes.

"Yes, Cousin Mabel," I answered. "I'm okay!"

All of a sudden, there was a tug and a twist and a crunchy sound and a "Hooray" from Mabel.

"Here it is!" she hollered.

She wet a washcloth and held it to my mouth. She opened the locked door and led me out into the kitchen.

"This boy needs some COLD ice cream," she announced. "He's just lost his first tooth!"

My first tooth and I were passed around so everyone could have a look.

My uncle Charles's best friend, Mickey Lynch, gave me a dime "in case the tooth fairy has the night off," he said, "what with the Easter Bunny coming and all."

I felt quite grown-up, but even so, I'd be sure to put my very first tooth under my pillow.

Chapter Ten

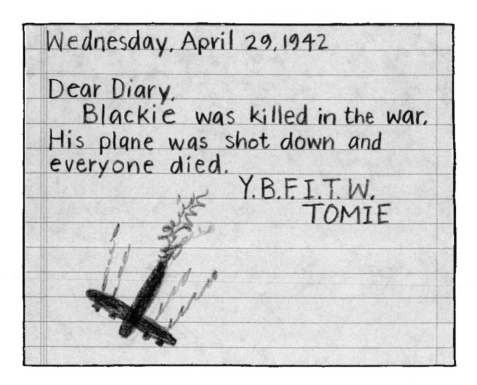

Wednesday, April 29, 1942

Dear Diary,
    Blackie was killed in the war.
His plane was shot down and
everyone died.
                        Y.B.F.I.T.W.
                            TOMIE

Dad has just come home from the Bronx in New York, where he had been to see Blackie's mother and father, Aunt Kate and Uncle Tony. I was sent up to bed, but I crept out into the upstairs hallway so I could listen.

I could hear Mom quietly crying.

"Oh, Joe, he was such a great young man, everything to live for. It's so sad, so sad," Mom said.

"I feel so sorry for Tony and Kate," Dad said. "It's the hardest thing to lose your first son, let alone ANY child. Kate's eyes have so much sorrow in them. I don't think she'll EVER be happy again."

I wondered if Dad was right. Then I began to wonder, *Why?*

Why was there a war anyway?

Why did the war make everything different when it was so far away?

Why did Uncle Charles have to go and be a soldier?

Why did Blackie's plane get shot down?

Why was my cousin Blackie, my cousin Anthony, who gave me a Hawaiian guitar and a hula skirt and who carried me on his back and listened to every new song I learned—why was Blackie dead?

WHY?

The End

26

Come home to **26 FAIRMOUNT AVENUE!**

26 Fairmount Avenue

a 2000 Newbery Honor Book

"A wonderful introduction to the art of the memoir." —*The Boston Globe*

★ "Effervescent . . . dePaola seems as at home in this format as he did when he first crossed the threshold of 26 Fairmount Avenue, an address readers will eagerly revisit in the series' subsequent tales."

—*Publishers Weekly* (starred review)

Here We All Are

★ "DePaola continues to share engaging childhood memories in this breezy follow-up to *26 Fairmount Avenue*." —*Publishers Weekly* (starred review)

On My Way

★ "DePaola is irresistible."

—*Kirkus Reviews* (starred review)

"DePaola's writing and recollective skills are so fresh that kids will feel like he's sitting right next to them." —*The Horn Book*

What a Year

"As charming and engaging as its predecessors."

—Kirkus Reviews

THE WAR YEARS

Things Will NEVER Be the Same

"The fifth installment in the series is delightful."

—School Library Journal

I'm Still Scared

★ "Utterly charming and believable. . . . A slice of real life, true in its history and emotional resonance."

—Kirkus Reviews (starred review)